D0603391

WARRIORS!
FIERCE FIGHTERS

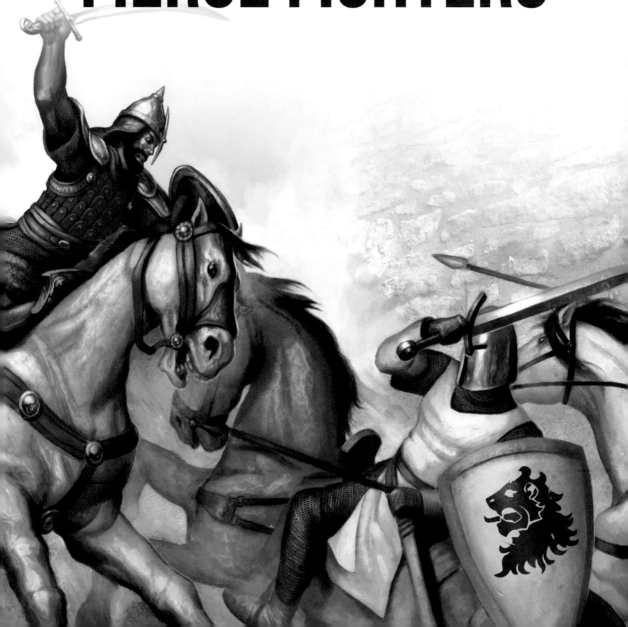

Thanks to the creative team:
Senior Editor: Alice Peebles
Design: www.collaborate.agency
Consultant: John Haywood

Original edition copyright 2015 by Hungry Tomato Ltd.

Copyright © 2016 by Lerner Publishing Group, Inc.

Hungry Tomato™ is a trademark of Lerner Publishing Group, Inc.

All rights reserved. International copyright secured. No part of this book may be reproduced, stored in a retrieval system, or transmitted in any form or by any means—electronic, mechanical, photocopying, recording, or otherwise—without the prior written permission of Lerner Publishing Group, Inc., except for the inclusion of brief quotations in an acknowledged review.

Hungry Tomato™
A division of Lerner Publishing Group, Inc.
241 First Avenue North
Minneapolis, MN 55401 USA

For reading levels and more information, look up this title at www.lernerbooks.com.
Main body text set in Bell MT.
Typeface provided by Monotype.

Library of Congress Cataloging-in-Publication Data

Chambers, Catherine, 1954–
 Fierce fighters / by Catherine Chambers ; illustrated by Jason Juta.
     pages cm. — (Warriors!)
 Includes bibliographical references and index.
 Audience: Ages 8-12.
 ISBN 978-1-4677-9357-5 (lb : alk. paper) — ISBN 978-1-4677-9599-9 (pb : alk. paper) — ISBN 978-1-4677-9600-2 (eb pdf)
 1. Generals—Biography—Juvenile literature. 2. Battles—Juvenile literature. I. Juta, Jason, illustrator. II. Title.
 D25.C43 2016
 355.0092'2—dc23

                         2015032763

Manufactured in the United States of America
1 – VP – 12/31/15

Discover more at **www.lernerbooks.com**

mbers, Catherine, 195
ce fighters /
6]
05234536740
11/04/16

WARRIORS!
FIERCE FIGHTERS

by Catherine Chambers
Illustrated by Jason Juta

HUNGRY
TOMATO™

CONTENTS

INTRODUCING MILITARY LEADERS

WHAT MAKES A MILITARY LEADER?

Some military leaders were the sons or daughters of kings and queens (such as Alexander the Great *[right]*, the son of King Phillip II of Macedonia), or of generals or famous warriors. They felt it was their duty to carry on wars begun by their parents. Some decided to do even better and further expand their territory. Most of these leaders were educated from a young age in the arts of warfare, weaponry, tactics, and the politics of their region.

Other military leaders seemed to spring up from nowhere. They rose because of a strong determination to defend or free their people. These leaders often became more ambitious and went on to increase their power and influence.

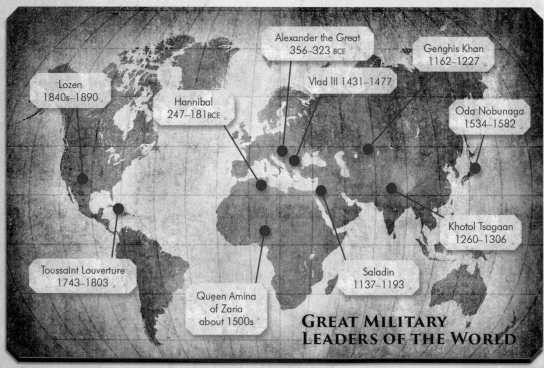

Alexander the Great
356–323 BCE

Genghis Khan
1162–1227

Vlad III 1431–1477

Lozen
1840s–1890

Hannibal
247–181 BCE

Oda Nobunaga
1534–1582

Khotol Tsagaan
1260–1306

Toussaint Louverture
1743–1803

Queen Amina
of Zaria
about 1500s

Saladin
1137–1193

GREAT MILITARY LEADERS OF THE WORLD

Why Go to War?

Some military leaders went to war to gain territory. This gave them more resources and control of new trade routes, making them wealthier. Others launched attacks to defend their territory and trade routes against aggressive neighbors. Some campaigned to defend their faith, others to expand their faith's influence. All these leaders used horrific methods to reach their goals.

Most of their gains did not last into modern times. But the impact of their conquests can be felt to this day, and they changed the course of history. For these mighty military leaders spread cultures and financial and political systems that we still recognize in the places that they conquered.

On the maps in this book, modern place-names are given to show where in the world these warrior leaders lived and fought.

What Did Great Military Leaders Say?

Military leaders did not have a lot of time to write in their diaries. These quotes are thought to be from some of the military leaders in this book.

Alexander the Great: "I am not afraid of an army of lions led by a sheep. I am afraid of an army of sheep led by a lion."

Hannibal: "We will either find a way or make one.'"

Genghis Khan: "If you are afraid, don't do it. If you are doing it, don't be afraid."

Genghis Khan

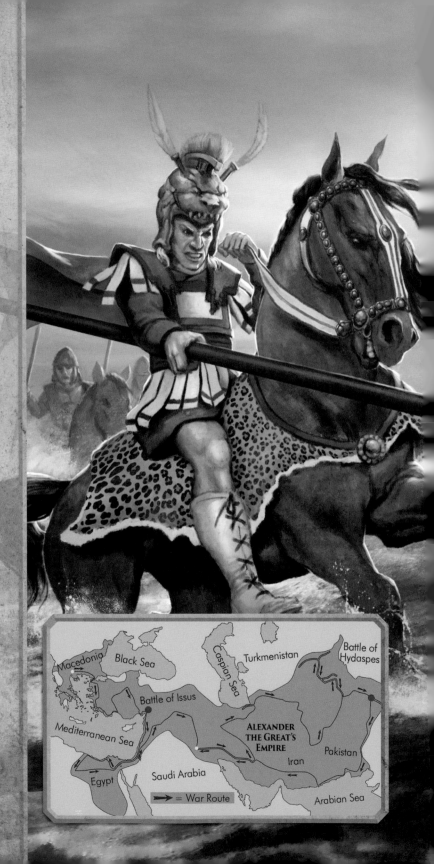

GREAT BATTLES

At the Battle of Issus in 333 BCE, Alexander charged straight through enemy lines at King Darius of Persia. Losing his nerve, Darius fled in his chariot, with his enormous army following behind.

TOP TACTICS

Alexander began an assault with an angled central column of foot soldiers, called *pezhetairoi*. He then led a cavalry charge on the right. A trusted general led another charge on the left.

TRUTH OR LEGEND?

In his lifetime, Alexander was seen as a god, the son of Zeus. Later, some said that he was the son of an Egyptian wizard-king; others said that in India he met Amazons, enormous women warriors.

FEROCIOUS FACTS

● Alexander's army looted and plundered, and killed children.

● His influence spread over 2 million square miles (5 million sq km).

● Some scientists say that Alexander was murdered by poisoning.

Macedonia Black Sea Caspian Sea Turkmenistan Battle of Hydaspes

Battle of Issus

Mediterranean Sea

ALEXANDER THE GREAT'S EMPIRE

Iran Pakistan

Egypt Saudi Arabia

➤ = War Route

Arabian Sea

ALEXANDER THE GREAT

Alexander of Macedonia led a terrifying army across ancient Greek states and east as far as India. His father, Philip, had left him a highly disciplined force, trained to use the 18-ft (5.5-m) sarissa. This spear was the longest used by any army, and it allowed Alexander's men to attack first. He always led his cavalry from the front, astride his beloved horse, Bucephalus. His infantry moved in a phalanx, a formation of tight rows. Alexander saw his enemy clearly and reacted quickly to their mistakes, while his daring inspired his own army to fight even harder.

WHERE
Kingdom of Macedonia – lands around the northwest Aegean Sea

WHEN
356–323 BCE

HANNIBAL

WHERE
Carthage,
North Africa

WHEN
247–about 181 BCE

Hannibal was a great North African general who used brilliant tactics to recapture lands from the Romans in the Second Punic War—though his own forces were much smaller. He used all means of transport, including 37 elephants, to cross the Pyrenees and Alps into the Roman heartland in Italy. Even there, Hannibal defeated the Romans, always using the terrain to his advantage. He forced them into valleys, stringing out their troops in lines that were hard to defend. He squeezed them against mountains and closed off access to food and water.

GREAT BATTLES

At the Battle of Trasimene (217 BCE), Hannibal hid his troops in a fog over Lake Trasimene. Roman troops moved toward them, and Hannibal's army drove thousands of them into the lake.

TOP TACTICS

Hannibal knew when his enemy was following him and at dusk led them into difficult positions. Then at night he placed his troops around the enemy and ambushed them in daylight.

TRUTH OR LEGEND?

Hannibal's deadly deeds were written by Romans! Did they portray him as superhuman to make his final defeat seem even greater? The origin of his elephants puzzles historians to this day.

FEROCIOUS FACTS

• In the Alps, Hannibal's engineers used fire and vinegar to break up huge rocks blocking their way.

• Hannibal's troops killed up to 70,000 Romans at the Battle of Cannae (216 BCE), his greatest victory.

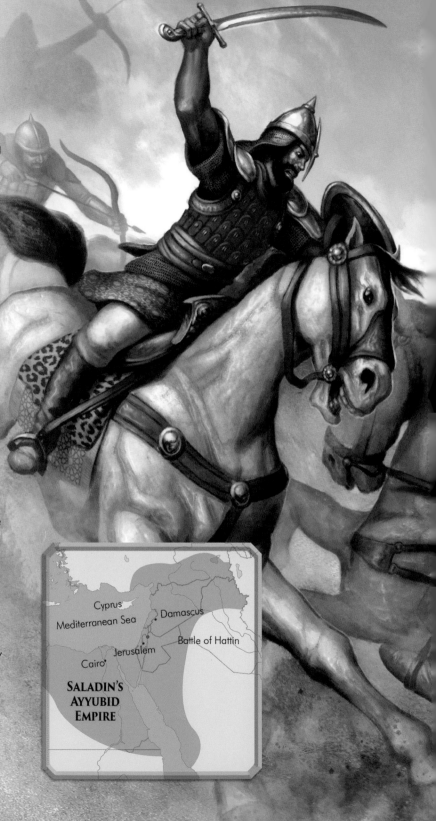

GREAT BATTLES

On October 2, 1187, Saladin finally ousted the Christian Franks from Jerusalem. He attacked the city walls with massive catapults. Saladin then dug down below one section, making it collapse.

TOP TACTICS

Saladin united the Arab commanders of small armies that were always fighting each other. He rallied them to fight for a common cause. Then he carefully chose battles that gave his cause the greatest advantage.

TRUTH OR LEGEND?

In legend, Saladin was honorable toward his enemies. He even offered gifts to one of his greatest foes, England's Richard the Lionheart. So far, historians say that all this is true.

FEROCIOUS FACTS

● Saladin terrified his enemy with gongs, trumpets, clashing cymbals, and yelling men.

● At the Battle of Hattin in 1187, Saladin executed most of the elite Christian military: the Knights Templar and Hospitallers.

Cyprus
Mediterranean Sea
Damascus
Battle of Hattin
Jerusalem
Cairo
SALADIN'S AYYUBID EMPIRE

SALADIN

Through stunning military skill, Saladin united Egypt, much of Syria, Yemen, and northern Iraq under his Ayyubid dynasty. He then tackled the Christian Crusaders who were competing with Muslims to rule the Holy Land, especially Jerusalem. Tactically, Saladin launched lightning strikes on the enemy's front and rear. His elite cavalries from Arab and Turkish or Bedouin and Nubian forces ram-raided and scattered the foe, firing arrows and javelins. They isolated enemy units, then surrounded and killed them with their short swords. The rest of the cavalry thundered in behind.

WHERE
Mesopotamia, now Iraq

WHEN
about 1137–1193

13

GENGHIS KHAN

WHERE
Mongolia

WHEN
1162–1227

Genghis Khan created the vast Mongol Empire by first uniting nomadic tribes on Asia's grassland steppes. He then moved with his swift cavalry to gain territory, from China in the east to Europe's Adriatic Sea in the west. Genghis Khan traveled with technical advisers and engineers. In his movable ger *(below)*, they spent months mapping the terrain he would cover. A favorite battle tactic was the false retreat before turning back suddenly on the enemy. Genghis Khan bombarded cities mercilessly, and he trampled and burned all before him so that the enemy could not rise again.

GENGHIS
KHAN'S
EMPIRE

Russia

Kazakhstan   Delun Boldog

Karakorum

Beijing

Bukhara

China

Hangzou

GREAT BATTLES

In the war against the great Persian Khwarezmid Empire (1218–1220), Genghis Khan sent in spies to threaten its citizens and divide its army. Then the slaughter began.

TOP TACTICS

Genghis Khan was a master of deception. He saddled straw soldiers on spare horses to make his cavalry seem larger. He lit many campfires to give the impression of a vast army.

TRUTH OR LEGEND?

In legend, Genghis Khan was born with a blood clot in his hand. His ancestor was a gray wolf! Some say these were signs of greatness; others, that they showed a ruthless genius.

FEROCIOUS FACTS

● Genghis Khan slaughtered friendly Mongolian nomad leaders, taking over their armies.

● He murdered any defeated Tatar (from an ancient Asiatic tribe) who was taller than the axle of a cart's wheel, leaving hordes of orphaned children.

GREAT BATTLES

Khutulun used spies, smokescreens, false retreats, ambushes, and lightning attacks against Kublai Khan. But she only managed to help her father to hold his own territory.

TOP TACTICS

Khutulun advised her father on which enemy to attack. Many Mongol rulers, including the great Genghis Khan, valued the tactical opinions of women.

TRUTH OR LEGEND?

Khutulun vowed to marry any man who could beat her at wrestling. Each man who lost had to give her 100 horses. Khutulun ended up with 10,000 horses!

FEROCIOUS FACTS

● Khutulun would leave her father's side, dash into the enemy, and return with a foe, dead or alive.

● She could even fight while riding her horse backward. Her 14 older brothers could not match her skills.

KHOTOL TSAGAAN

A descendant of Genghis Khan, Khotol Tsagaan was the daughter of Kaidu, ruler of Mongolia and Turkestan. She was also known as Khutulun and took part in her father's later fierce battles against his brother, Kublai Khan of China. Khutulun's smart battle tactics, psychological warfare and political knowledge of the region made her essential to her father's campaigns. Her riding and archery skills were second to none. A famous Italian travel writer, Marco Polo, described Khutulun as big and strong. She could snatch up an enemy as easily as a hawk snatches a bird.

WHERE
Turkestan and Mongolia

WHEN
about 1260–1306

VLAD III

WHERE
Principality of
Wallachia in present-
day Romania

WHEN
1431–about 1477

Vlad III fought savagely to regain and retain Wallachia, once ruled by his father. At times he made enemies of nearby Hungarians or powerful Ottoman Turks. At other times he cunningly sought each as allies. This terrifying prince was also known as Vlad Dracula, Vlad Tepes, and Vlad the Impaler. His tactic of impaling the enemy on rows of sharpened sticks gave him the last two names. Vlad organized his small army well, using ambush, night attacks, sabotage, and other guerrilla tactics.

GREAT BATTLES

Vlad tried to push the Ottomans toward the River Danube. But the Ottoman army was three times greater than his own. Still, he impaled 20,000 enemy troops and freed Wallachia, for a while.

TOP TACTICS

Vlad often invited rivals to feast at his court. Then he murdered them. He first used this tactic on nobles whom he suspected of betraying his father to Hungarian troops.

TRUTH OR LEGEND?

Folk tales relate that Vlad executed between 40,000 and 100,000 captives. The numbers may not be true, but he probably did publicly torture, maim, and execute many.

FEROCIOUS FACTS

● Vlad severed his enemies' arms, legs, and noses.

● He left his maimed captives out in the cold to be devoured by wolves.

EUROPE Hungary

Romania

Ottoman Turkish Empire

Transylvania

VLAD III'S WALLACHIA, NOW IN MODERN ROMANIA

GREAT BATTLES

Queen Amina swept southward for hundreds of miles, crushing and controlling greater kingdoms, such as Nupe and Jukun. Her greatest assets were her swift horses, imported at great expense from lands north of the Sahara.

TOP TACTICS

Queen Amina surrounded her military camps with protective ditches and high, gated walls. She defended Zaria city in this way, too. The walls can be seen to this day.

TRUTH OR LEGEND?

Was Queen Amina born a warrior? Legend tells that she loved fighting, even as a small child. It is said that her grandmother caught her clutching a dagger as a toddler.

FEROCIOUS FACTS

● Amina used her cutlass skillfully to slash the iron helmets and chain mail of her more powerful rivals.

● It is said that she picked a captured soldier every night and murdered him.

20

QUEEN AMINA OF ZARIA

With her superb tactics, Queen Amina increased the power and wealth of Zaria, a city kingdom of the Hausa people. From the age of 16 she led her cavalry across West Africa's Sahel grasslands. Horses were rare in this area and gave Amina a great military advantage. For 34 years she subdued other, greater Hausa kingdoms. Her influence extended over 2,000 miles (3,200 km) westward to the Atlantic Ocean. She forced all defeated powers to pay to continue trading across the Sahara. This trade in salt, gold, potash, leather goods, livestock, and slaves led to Zaria's greatness.

WHERE
Zazzau, now Zaria, northern Nigeria

WHEN
About 1500s

Algeria

Libya

Mali

Niger

Chad

QUEEN AMINA CONTROLLED TRADE ROUTES SOUTH OF THE SAHARA

Nigeria

Zaria

Major Overland Trade Routes in the 1500s

ODA NOBUNAGA

WHERE
Owari, Japan

WHEN
1534–1582

Oda Nobunaga was determined to be more powerful than his minor warlord father and ended up uniting half the feudal states of Japan. Nobunaga defeated armies far stronger than his own, using ambush, daring attacks, and a new weapon, the musket, imported from Europe. With these muskets, savage swords, spears, and his tight, disciplined units, Nobunaga first united Owari province. Then he tackled other provinces until he reached the capital, Kyoto, securing the vital seaport of Osaka. Nobunaga established a strong economy in every territory that he gained. This gave him the wealth to continue his battles.

ODA NOBUNAGA'S EMPIRE

East Japan

Central Japan

West Japan

GREAT BATTLES

At the Battle of Okehazama in 1560, Nobunaga's 3,000 troops faced 25,000 commanded by the great Imagawa Yoshimoto. With stealth, and aided by a distracting thunderstorm, Nobunaga ambushed them in a gorge.

TOP TACTICS

Nobunaga used deceit and decoys to confuse and trap his enemy in difficult terrain. He made dummy soldiers from straw, topped with helmets. Then he flew flags among them.

TRUTH OR LEGEND?

Some say Nobunaga was a demon king because he ruthlessly burned people alive. Others say that he was seen as evil only after his death. Nobunaga saw himself as a living god.

FEROCIOUS FACTS

- Nobunaga ruthlessly burned Buddhist monasteries outside Kyoto and slaughtered the powerful warrior monks.

- In 1574 he set fire to an enemy fortress at Nagashima, massacring 20,000 men, women, and children inside.

GREAT BATTLES

Toussaint first fought alongside the British to rid St. Domingue of its French rulers. But the British later became his enemy, and in 1800 Toussaint defeated them in seven battles over seven days.

TOP TACTICS

Toussaint spread his units out over thick forest. There, he waited patiently for the enemy. He then drew his units in around his foe, surrounding and finally attacking them.

TRUTH OR LEGEND?

In legend, Toussaint's father was Gaou-Ginou, a chieftain from the Arada people of West Africa. This tale gave him high status—but in reality his father was probably an educated slave called Pierre Baptiste Simon.

FEROCIOUS FACTS

• Toussaint's troops burned sugar plantations and murdered hated slave owners. Toussaint saved the less brutal owners.

• Farm-tool weapons included vicious cane-cutting machete knives.

• Toussaint killed Spanish churchgoers who were attending Mass.

TOUSSAINT LOUVERTURE'S CARIBBEAN

Atlantic Ocean

Cuba

Caribbean Sea

Jamaica

Haiti

Dominican Republic

Puerto Rico

TOUSSAINT LOUVERTURE

Toussaint Louverture was the inspiring leader of the only successful slave revolt in the Americas. Toussaint was a freed slave on St. Domingue, a French colony on the west side of the island of Hispaniola. In 1791 he joined freedom fighters to rid St. Domingue of its brutal sugar plantation slave owners and the French. Toussaint used stealth to spot gaps in his enemy's defenses, and the terrain to stalk and ambush his foe. His first weapons were farming tools, cutlasses, and pointed sticks. After freeing St. Domingue, Toussaint defeated invading British troops and the Spanish rulers of Hispaniola's east side.

WHERE
St. Domingue, now Haiti, on Hispaniola Island, Caribbean

WHEN
1743–1803

LOZEN

WHERE
Chiricahua Apache
homelands, USA

WHEN
Late 1840s–1890

Lozen fought with guile and strength to defend her people, the Chiricahua Apache, against the forces of the United States, who had taken their lands. She joined her brother Victorio's band to strike at both US and Mexican troops. Lozen located them from far away, waiting in high crags overlooking trails. Using her knowledge of the landscape, she then surrounded and ambushed them. Lozen could train any horse and ride it up rocky mountains and across raging rivers. She was lethal with a rifle and a knife. Yet, despite her great warrior's skills, Lozen could not free her people.

Colorado River

Rio Grande

Arizona

CHIRICAHUA
APACHE
HOMELANDS

New Mexico

Gila River

Mexico

GREAT BATTLES

After Victorio's death, Lozen joined Geronimo, the famous Apache warrior. In one battle, he ran out of ammunition. So Lozen crawled toward enemy fire and stole a stash of bullets.

TOP TACTICS

Lozen built decoy camps to trick the enemy. Her superb survival skills meant that she knew when her foe was weakened by lack of food and water.

TRUTH OR LEGEND?

In legend, young Lozen climbed the Sacred Mountain (Salinas Peak) to receive special powers from the spirits. She returned with a mystical sense that helped her locate the Chiricahua Apache's enemies.

FEROCIOUS FACTS

- Victorio said, "Lozen is my right hand...strong as a man, braver than most, and cunning in strategy."
- In 1879, Victorio's band killed eight people in US Captain Ambrose's camp and stole 46 horses.

FAMOUS BATTLES

ALEXANDER THE GREAT AND THE BATTLE OF HYDASPES RIVER (326 BCE)

Alexander had swept through Greece, Egypt, the Middle East, and Persia. Now it was time to tackle India and beyond. His main obstacle was King Porus, who held an area now in Pakistan's Panjab region. Alexander surprised his foe by crossing the River Jhelum in full monsoon flood to face him. King Porus commanded a mighty army of infantry, cavalry, and towering elephants. It was three times larger than Alexander's force, but Alexander's tactics were superior. His cavalry launched a storm of arrows that attacked Porus's left side, while his pikemen pushed back the elephants. Finally, Alexander sent his other generals to attack the enemy's rear and surround King Porus's army.

HANNIBAL AND THE BATTLE OF CANNAE (216 BCE)

Hannibal and his army had crossed the Pyrenees mountains and the towering Alps, defeating bands of fierce-fighting tribes all the way. Now he faced the Romans at the village of Cannae. About 80,000 Roman troops advanced confidently, the sea behind them and the River Aufidus to their right. They pushed forward with most of their troops in a long line, thinking that this would relentlessly crush Hannibal's 50,000 soldiers. Hannibal deployed his Gallic and Spanish troops in the center, Africans at their sides, and cavalry on their wings, in a crescent shape. As the Romans moved forward, Hannibal's crescent encircled and trapped them, defeating them heavily.

Saladin and the Battle of Hattin (1187)

Saladin had made a truce with the Christian Crusader states. It was broken, though, by Reginald of Chatillon. This French Crusader had attacked Muslim trading caravans crossing the Holy Land. It was now all-out war. Saladin attacked the city of Tiberias on the west side of the Sea of Galilee. The Crusaders were camped about 20 miles (32 km) from Galilee and decided to march toward their enemy. But they grew weak from thirst and Saladin's cavalry strikes. Saladin used this advantage to pin the Crusaders back to two great hills, the Horns of Hattin. The Crusaders were slaughtered, and Saladin himself took the life of Reginald of Chatillon.

Genghis Khan's Xixia Campaign, China (1205–1210)

Genghis Khan wanted to attack the great Jin Empire to the north of the Yangtze River. But he knew that he must first defeat the northwestern state of Xixia. If he did not, the Xixia might hit his flank as he drove toward Jin. So, after a few quick assaults to unsettle the Xixia, he launched a full invasion. In 1209 Genghis and his troops trekked across the Gobi Desert and smashed the Xixia's Wolohai fortress. He then led his cavalry over high mountains to the capital, Yinchuan. Here he made a false retreat, drawing out Xixia troops and capturing their commander. Yinchuan surrendered after Genghis flooded it with water—which also rushed down and flooded his own troops!

Vlad III's Night Attack (June 17, 1462)

Vlad III had impaled thousands of Turks, angering Mehmet II, ruler of Turkey. So Vlad was faced with Mehmet's 300,000 troops, which vastly outnumbered his own. At the River Danube, Vlad met Mehmet's army in a brief clash. He then retreated to Targoviste, Wallachia's capital. As he marched, Vlad poisoned wells and burned food stores to starve Mehmet's oncoming troops. He also ordered stealth attacks on them. Then, in the dead of night on June 17, Vlad launched an all-out attack on Mehmet's camp, slaughtering thousands.

MORE FEROCIOUS FACTS

- Alexander the Great let nothing get in his way. He completely wiped out a top Greek enemy unit called the Sacred Band of Thebes. At Persepolis, he burned down a Persian palace in revenge for a defeat 100 years earlier!

- Lozen fought more battles for the Chiricahua Apache than any other fighter, including the great Geronimo and even her brother Victorio. She would locate the enemy by praying alone in the desert. She kept turning around until she felt a trembling sensation in her hands, which indicated the direction and strength of her foe.

- To this day, Queen Amina of Zaria is called "Amina, daughter of Nikatau, a woman as capable as a man." In fact her military gains were far greater than her father's, and she was as smart in defense as in attack.

- Vlad III surrounded his castle with a forest of spikes to impale traitors, invaders, or even innocent people to terrorize his enemies. Sometimes he arranged the spikes in geometric patterns to entertain himself.

- Lozen once left Victorio's band to rescue a mother with her new baby. First she braved gunfire to steal a Mexican cavalry horse for the mother to ride. She also stole a cowboy's horse and a soldier's rifle and ammunition for herself. Then she led the mother to safety.

- Genghis Khan used his siege machines to catapult hot boulders, bombs, and dead, decaying, and diseased animals into enemy strongholds. He hoped they would infect the enemy.

- Oda Nobunaga did not hesitate to murder his own family members. These included his uncle Nobutomo and his uncle Shiba Yoshimune. With these two men out of the way, Nobunaga was able to take control of Owari province.

- Two foreign ambassadors visited Vlad III's court and refused to remove their hats politely in his presence. So Vlad ordered his guards to nail their hats to their heads.

GLOSSARY

CAVALRY
Soldiers on horseback

COLONY
A nation ruled by an invading country

DECOY
Something used to distract and confuse the enemy

FLANK
The right or left side of an armed unit

GER
A round Mongolian tent made of felt or skins, also called a yurt

GUERRILLA
A tactic against a larger force using speed and stealth

IMPALE
To spike with a sharpened stake

INFANTRY
Foot soldiers

MACHETE
A long, flat, sharp-bladed cutlass

MAIM
To injure so that the victim cannot use their body well

MUSKET
A firearm loaded through the front end, or muzzle

PEZHETAIROI
Alexander the Great's column of foot soldiers bearing spears and shields

PIKEMAN
A soldier wielding any type of spear

PLUNDER
To take food, goods, and treasure in an attack

RESERVATION
A fenced-in land in which a group of people are forced to live

SABOTAGE
Deliberate destruction to hinder an enemy's plans

SAHEL
A region in West Africa between the Sahara in the north and a forest region to the south

SARISSA
A long, sharp javelin or pike developed in ancient Greece

SIEGE WEAPON
A huge, strong weapon that can batter defensive walls

INDEX

THE AUTHOR

Catherine Chambers was born in Adelaide, South Australia, grew up in the UK, and studied African history and Swahili at the School of Oriental and African Studies in London. She has written about 130 books for children and young adults and enjoys seeking out intriguing facts for her nonfiction titles, which cover history, cultures, faiths, biography, geography, and the environment.

THE ILLUSTRATOR

Jason Juta is a South-African born illustrator living in London. He studied graphic design but turned to illustration and works in two styles. He creates fantasy art for the gaming industry (*Dungeons and Dragons* and *Star Wars*, for example) by using 3-D to work out perspective, and personal work based on photography, with dark, mythic themes, painted in a traditional way.

Picture Credits (abbreviations: t = top; b = bottom; c = center; l = left; r = right)
© www.shutterstock.com: 6 tl, 6 bc, 7 cl
7 br Daniel Prudek / Shutterstock.com